Remodeled
Kitchens & Baths
Dramatic Makeovers

Before

Before

Tina Skinner & Melissa Cardona

Schiffer Publishing Ltd

4880 Lower Valley Road, Atglen, PA 19310 USA

M000169981

Acknowledgments

Many thanks to all our contributors, who provided photographs, floorplans, project descriptions, and anything else we needed to complete this book. We sincerely appreciate your help. As always, thanks to all the photographers for beautifully capturing these amazing kitchen and bath designs.

Photography Credits:

Cover: Courtesy of Kitchens by Kleweno/Photography by Steve Sanders

Page 1: Courtesy of Cheryl A. Van Duyne, ASID/Photography by Ira Montgomery

Page 1 inset: Courtesy of Showplace Design & Remodeling, Inc./Photography by Roger Turk, Northlight Photography, Inc.

Page 3: Courtesy of Joseph Hittinger Designs/Photography by Bernardo Grijalva

Back Cover: Courtesy of Design Christian Huebner Interiors, Inc./Photography Mark Sinclair

Library of Congress Cataloging-in-Publication Data:

Skinner, Tina.
    Remodeling kitchens & baths : dramatic makeovers / by Tina Skinner & Melissa Cardona.
        p. cm.
    ISBN 0-7643-2138-2 (pbk.)
1. Kitchens—Remodeling—Amateurs' manual. 2. Kitchens—Remodeling—Amateurs' manual. I. Cardona, Melissa. II. Title.

TH4816.3.K58S52 2005
747.7'97—dc22
                                    2004025677

Designed by John P. Cheek
Cover design by John P. Cheek
Type set in Enviro D/AvanteGarde Md BT/Humanist 521 Lt BT

ISBN: 0-7643-2138-2
Printed in China

Published by Schiffer Publishing Ltd.
4880 Lower Valley Road
Atglen, PA 19310
Phone: (610) 593-1777; Fax: (610) 593-2002
E-mail: Info@schifferbooks.com

For the largest selection of fine reference books on this and related subjects, please visit our web site at www.schifferbooks.com
We are always looking for people to write books on new and related subjects. If you have an idea for a book please contact us at the above address.

This book may be purchased from the publisher.
Include $3.95 for shipping.
Please try your bookstore first.
You may write for a free catalog.

In Europe, Schiffer books are distributed by
Bushwood Books
6 Marksbury Ave.
Kew Gardens
Surrey TW9 4JF England
Phone: 44 (0) 20 8392-8585; Fax: 44 (0) 20 8392-9876
E-mail: info@bushwoodbooks.co.uk
Free postage in the U.K., Europe; air mail at cost.

Contents

Before You Begin

First thing's first when you're planning a remodeling project, and the first thing, like it or not, is always money. Before you fall in love with those custom designed cabinets or that Sub Zero refrigerator, create a budget for yourself. Depending on the scope of your project, the cost of renovating a bathroom can start at $7,000 – if you do all the work yourself – and rise quickly with upgrades on materials, fixtures, and paid help. Kitchen projects normally entail a set of brand new cabinets and can run you anywhere from $20,000 at the low end of the scale. Most projects tend to go over budget, so give your bank account some leeway by planning to spend less than what you can reasonably afford. Your pockets will thank you later.

Once you've drawn the bottom line, you can start deciding what you need and want in your kitchen or bath. How you use those rooms now should help you determine what changes need to be made there. Start thinking about what works and what doesn't in the existing space. Is the showerhead too low in your bathroom? Do you have somewhere to keep towels and extra toiletries? Is there enough workspace in the kitchen? Do your guests have somewhere to sit when you entertain? Common problems include outdated appliances and fixtures, inadequate lighting and storage, and an inconvenient layout. Determine necessary changes that need to be made, keeping in mind that any structural modifications will inflate the cost of a project significantly. Then you can decide what you want – but don't necessarily need – taking care to rank those items in case you have to trim costs. After you've decided which functional aspects of your kitchen or bath you'd like to change, you can begin thinking about the look of the room and start choosing materials, color schemes, and décor items.

If you decide that a major renovation project isn't right for you, or your pocketbook, at the moment, there are many options for upgrading kitchens and baths without great expense. You can create a whole new look for your bathroom simply by changing the hardware, faucets, and commode, and by installing new mirrors or medicine cabinets. Results can be very dramatic, the cost minimal. Likewise, there are options for improving the look of your kitchen without spending too much money or time. Paint can work wonders in the kitchen, especially on a good set of sturdy cabinets. Adding new hardware, fixtures, and backsplashes can also dramatically change a kitchen's look, and are relatively easy do-it-yourself projects.

This book contains both the high-end projects that feature the best options in kitchen and bathroom amenities, along with projects that were completed on a budget. Either way, you'll be inspired by the changes, big and small, that were made to improve the function and look of the spaces featured. These case studies will help you decide what changes are necessary in your home, and shed light on the possibilities for remodeling projects.

Refer to the list of contributors in the back of the book and call one in your area. If you're planning a large project, these designers, architects, and contractors can help streamline the process and maybe even cut costs. They are the experts, after all, and will ensure that your kitchen or bath is transformed into the room of your dreams. Share this book and your favorite projects with them to give them a better idea of what you want for your own project – including features, appliances, materials, and style. Enjoy!

Courtesy of Plain & Fancy Custom Cabinetry
Photography: Simone Associates, Lebanon, PA

A Pro Shares Her Personal Experience

Jackie Depew, ASID, operates her own interior design business in Austin, Texas. Yet when she turned her attentions, and amateur carpentry skills, toward her own little pet project, the results were simply delightful. She shares her experience in turning a second home into a charming retreat, while cutting corners on cost and labor:

"In the summer of 2002, my husband and I bought a small, one-bedroom/one bath home on Lake LBJ in the Texas hill country. We bought it with the idea of remodeling and adding on to it, so the first thing required was an enlarged septic system to handle the addition. Frustrated at sinking money into something I could not see (the septic), I turned to making the existing spaces more functional and cheerful.

"There were several problems to be addressed in the remodel. Whenever we had a large group, or even just our whole family, there were inadequate cooking and serving areas, storage, and a space to get drinks (coffee, tea, soft drinks) out of the way of the cooking area. New cabinets solved these problems. Also, with only one bathroom and being at a lake, there was never enough room for all the towels.

"The kitchen was gutted…and we decided to test our own skills at cabinetry and bought units from Home Depot that we assembled and hung. I'll never do that again! Since we only worked on the cabinets on weekends, it took over three months to complete them.

Festive décor is among the draws for a family who weekends at this little, lakeside home. Minor adjustments have made the home much more livable as the owners await a planned expansion of the small house.

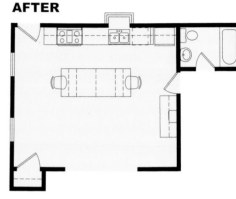

Opposite page:
Towels were of tantamount importance for the only bathroom in this family vacation home. Not only for showering, but for heading down to the lake. Bright and varied designs were chosen to help everyone identify their towels.

Meanwhile, the kitchen was totally out of commission. My husband found a stove on eBay that he purchased for $1, and we had it and a dishwasher from another home painted cobalt blue. We were on our way!

"The tile backsplashes are a reflection of the wildlife, fish, plants and terrain around our home on the lake and also include things our family loves: fried chicken, bacon and eggs, a black lab, donkeys, deer, etc. The tiles are a definite conversation piece with everyone who visits our home. They all came from Architerra, a tile showroom in Austin that represents many artist studios.

"In the bathroom, the only original thing that remains is the toilet. The space is small, so we eliminated the heavy oak sink and medicine cabinets. We added beaded board and bright, cheerful spring green paint. The medicine cabinet/mirror serves the purpose as does the much smaller pedestal lavatory. The solution to all of the wet towels on the floor was the addition of a whole row of robe hooks. Instead of bath towels, we use colorful beach towels, each with a different design, so everyone can remember which towel is their's. The black-and-white checkered flooring added the right touch of spunk to this small bathroom.

"We've solved many of the problems, and many are yet to be conquered, but we can now enjoy our small lake home even more."

Stretched Out

Too small for the homeowners' needs, this kitchen afforded minimal seating and outdated appliances. The space was increased and the layout rearranged to provide more storage, seating, and a more comfortable breakfast nook. The additional space also allowed for the construction of a pantry and closet in the new kitchen.

Alder wood cabinets in a custom scrubbed caramel finish, granite countertops in Santa Fe brown, a stone tile and hardwood floor, and new stainless steel appliances helped to bring this kitchen into the 21st century.

BEFORE

BEFORE

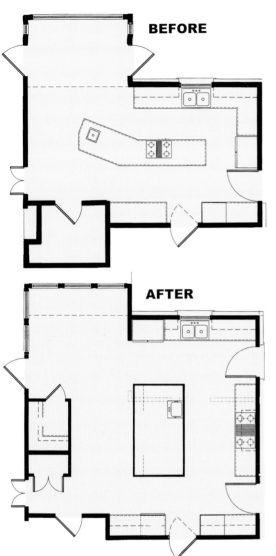

AFTER

◈ The exterior wall of the kitchen was pushed out 16' into the backyard. This created much more spacious work and breakfast areas.

◈ An awkwardly shaped island was replaced by a rectangular island with bar top seating. The new island created more space in the passageway that led to the breakfast area.

Design: Harrison Design Associates
Design Galleria Kitchen & Bath Studio

All that Remains

BEFORE

Two attractive glass-front cabinets remain as the only reminders of the former kitchen design in this home. Cleaned up and repainted to match new cabinetry, they continue to serve as centerpieces framing a sink and window. Today the kitchen sports a central island, and a wall of pantry storage that was created by borrowing a little less than a foot of wall space from an extra large powder room on the other side. The homeowner, in this case, is quite tall, and enjoys cooking while entertaining. The kitchen bar was built at 42" tall – the standard bar height – and intended as a place where people would hang out during a party.

Because the owner is tall, a drawer/wall cabinet combination worked along the outside wall, while double wall cabinets are utilized elsewhere. Along the pantry wall and island, a row of waist-high drawers creates a wonderful repeat pattern.

◈The island is topped with granite, while tile surrounds it on three counters and underfoot. The various textures add interest to a room dominated by neutral cream colors.

◈ An arched frame outlines the range area, and mirrors the original glass-front cabinets flanking the sink.

BEFORE

Design: Galya Jett Shannon, ASID / Inside Incorporated
Photography: Billy Stone

On a Mission

A kitchen with no style, poor quality cabinets, and outdated appliances motivated these homeowners to renovate it. The couple wanted enough space so they could both work in the kitchen at the same time, while keeping guests out of the prep area. The updated kitchen features more storage space, a more elegant look, and an ambiance that reflects the Spanish mission style of the home.

Rustic chocolate glaze cabinetry, hand-tooled copper hood, copper plumbing fixtures, inlaid mosaic backsplash with copper clavo details, copper hardware, and stone faux painted walls all define and support the home's Spanish mission style.

AFTER

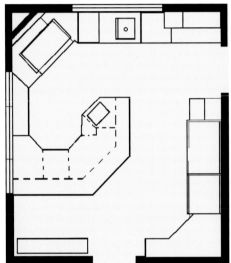

◈ An existing window was replaced by a shorter one to allow for wrap-around cabinetry with full-extension, extra wide drawers for added storage capacity.

◈ A 45-degree angle layout was chosen to provide visual interest, and to help keep guests out the prep area.

Design: Sharon Daroca / Design 2 Interiors, Inc.
Patrice Greene / Dzign-It
Photography: Jeffrey Cree

A Natural Change

BEFORE

As part of an extensive remodel of an island home nestled at the water's edge, the homeowners wanted to enhance the function and aesthetics of their kitchen in a style consistent with the home's original design. The clients' desired changes included increasing ambient and natural light; integrating the kitchen, nook, and family room; and increasing storage. In keeping with the interior's original style, characterized by natural materials like slate floors and cedar paneling, warm, natural woods were introduced into the kitchen to enhance the elegantly rustic look.

◈ Space was limited to the confines of the existing floorplan with minor modifications. A wall between the nook and family room hid a stunning view and limited the amount of light admitted to the rooms. The wall was reduced to a pony wall, allowing the homeowners to take advantage of the great waterfront views.

◈ Removing a soffit that limited the height of the cabinets allowed space to stagger 42" wall cabinets to increase storage.

◈ Stripping the wide-plank pegged oak floors revealed the natural beauty of the wood and enhanced the contrast of the darker pegs, while further lightening the space.

The introduction of warm cherry cabinets with recessed panels added warmth and beauty to this kitchen. Contrasting dark trim was included to add interest and complement the granite slab countertops.

BEFORE　　　　　　　　**AFTER**

The original faux brick backsplash was replaced with
honed limestone accentuated with polished onyx mosaics.

Design: Sheila Tilander, AKBD / Showplace Design & Remodeling, Inc.
Photography: Roger Turk / Northlight Photography, Inc.

Opening Up

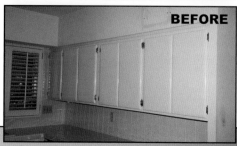

BEFORE

A cramped, U-shaped kitchen could only accommodate one person at a time. Opening up the area to the dining room drastically altered the amount of space, and created room for a new, luxurious kitchen.

◇ A work island adds the additional counter space needed in a home with more than one enthusiastic cook.

Open cabinets on the work island create a place for books and accessories to be displayed. The black furniture piece was built in to look like a found piece, and is used as an accent.

Design: Patricia Coats / Kitchens by Design of Sarasota
Photography: Lionel Murphy

Open to Change

Inspired by the gracious feeling of this Victorian home, an outdated kitchen was transformed into an open, inviting space for a family fond of entertaining. Comfort and functionality were the main goals of the woman of the household, who spends a lot of time cooking, but she also wanted the new design to blend with the home's Victorian interior.

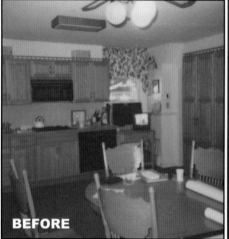

BEFORE

BEFORE

This outdated kitchen was an impractical space for owners who loved to cook and entertain. Limited counter space made for crowded cooking, and only two overhead lights did little to brighten the room.

◈ A bathroom was removed to make space for a new wet bar, and to completely open up the kitchen to the adjoining family room.

◈ What was once the back entrance into the kitchen became the entry into a light-filled sunroom addition. To make room for a large, light-giving opening, the refrigerator was moved to the opposite wall.

◈ A stairway leading to the second floor was repositioned to further open up the space and make room for the breakfast table.

◈ An island was added to facilitate easier cooking prep for the chef of the house, who also requested a full size refrigerator and freezer, and a double oven. To save valuable counter space, the second oven was placed in the reconfigured butler's pantry.

A custom stucco hood is the focal point of the renovated kitchen, which boasts lots of light. A beautiful hanging fixture, recessed spotlights, halogen lighting beneath the cabinetry, and lights in glass cabinets all work on dimmers, so lighting can be customized to the moment's need.

Design: L.D. Burke Designs
Photography: Rosemary Carroll

The removal of a powder room opened up the space for this wet bar, which features a wine cooler. The wall cabinetry that flanks the opening to the sunroom includes double-sided glass doors and open backsplashes to take advantage of the natural light by letting it into the kitchen.

Custom-made cherry wood cabinets with a mahogany stain replaced the outdated originals. The island was a necessary addition for these homeowners, who love to entertain. Here, the cook can easily mingle with guests as they sip wine and savor hors d'oeuvres before sitting down to dinner.

BEFORE

AFTER

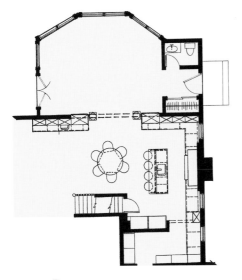

Hand carved decorative corbels, valance mouldings, and rope pilasters add elegance and a touch of the Old World. Niches on the side of the custom hood provide space for the cook's favorite spices.

Polished granite countertops and tumbled marble tile add luxury to the kitchen.

Attaining Enlightenment

This dark and dingy kitchen was split in half by an awkwardly placed staircase and needed a complete overhaul. The owner, and designer, wanted a kitchen that radiated sophisticated country charm and maintained functionality. Keeping the original antiqued brass hood, the entire kitchen was dramatically changed to be brighter, warmer, and more practical.

BEFORE

The designer and owner of this kitchen wanted a brighter, warmer kitchen. He decided to cover the walls in an historic reproduction pattern in burnt orange to complement the charming country look he wanted to achieve.

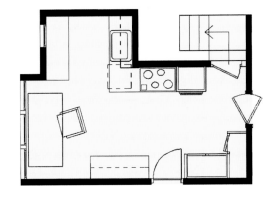

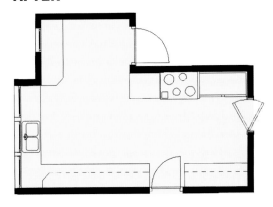

An antique brass hood was the only salvaged remnant from the original kitchen.

◈ By reorienting the back staircase to hide behind the back wall, the kitchen became one whole room.

◈ Hardwood floors were installed and finished with a warm ebony stain, also used on the new base cabinets.

◈ White marble was used to cover the base cabinets and for the backsplash behind the stove. White cabinets and warm white trim and ceiling were chosen to carry light around the room.

◈ Strategically placed spotlights were installed to provide task lighting.

White marble countertops reflect and enhance the light from the room's only window.

Design: Miller / Dolezal Design Group
Photography: www.davidduncanlivingston.com

25

Professional Grade

A professional chef wanted his kitchen to function and look as well as he was able to cook. The design goal of this project was to try and fit large-scale items required by a chef into the existing space, as well as to maximize storage and efficient work areas, while maintaining an attractive aesthetic. With no structural changes to the existing kitchen and the introduction of larger windows and cabinetry, the renovated space manages to feel more spacious, and much more sophisticated.

BEFORE

A custom marble and stainless steel island with a sink dramatically increases the perceptible size of the kitchen by leaving open floor space. Only high-end, professional grade appliances were used in this stylish kitchen.

◈ An existing peninsula that separated the kitchen from the breakfast nook was removed from the new design, greatly opening up the space.

◈ The original windows were replaced with larger ones to let in more light.

◈ Filling the space to its capacity with some cabinets climbing to the ceiling had the effect of making it seem larger.

BEFORE

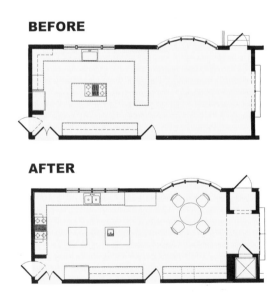

AFTER

Design: Harrison Design Associates

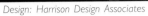

Beauty on a Budget

One of the functional goals of this remodeling project was to reorganize the circulation from the back door through the eating nook, and to provide a storage bench and hooks for coats, boots, and bags. Another goal of the project was to open up the view from the kitchen to the outdoors, better connecting the room to the patio. Reusing the existing gas range, surface mounting the kitchen's new lighting, and maintaining the existing cabinet and plumbing layout helped to minimize costs and stay within a budget.

BEFORE

The new color palette of this kitchen is a natural extension of the warm wood tones of the cabinets and cool finish of the stainless steel appliances and countertops.

BEFORE

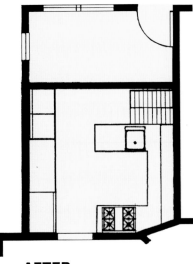

AFTER

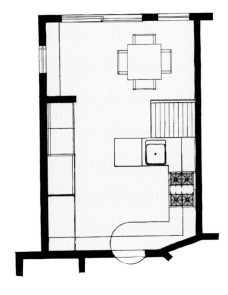

◈ The opening between the kitchen and the dining room was enlarged and a counter with seating was added.

◈ New treads and a handrail were installed on the existing stairs to the loft. The original bulky wood railing was replaced by a sleeker cable rail to open up the space.

◈ Cabinets were designed to maximize storage, including the addition of a pantry, laundry supply storage, and open shelving for display. The use of cabinet doors with ribbed glass helped to create the sense of more space, as did their taller dimensions.

Design: Torrell Architects
Photography: R. Lauris Bitners

Expanded Horizons

The kitchen in a 1926 California Mission-style house was badly in need of a makeover. It had not been renovated since a 1960s remodel. The owners cited inadequate and dated cabinetry, lack of natural light, and old appliances as motivation to update the space, not to mention the buttercup yellow wallpaper and linoleum flooring. Adding several feel to the end and one side of the kitchen dramatically improved the way space could be used, and made room for modern amenities, which took up more space than the '60s orignals.

BEFORE

BEFORE

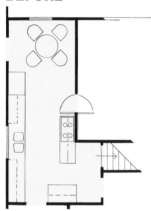

AFTER

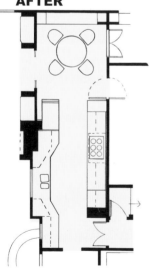

Cherry cabinets, granite countertops, and wood floors create an inviting and beautiful atmosphere. Hand-made Mexican tiles were chosen to complement the home's Mission-style.

◈ The kitchen was gutted. Eight feet were added to the breakfast nook area, and the sink-side wall of the room was pushed back several feet to accommodate the larger-size modern cabinetry.

◈ Architectural soffiting was done to reflect the existing soft-edged stucco walls in the house.

◈ Bigger, new steel windows were installed to match the original windows, while letting in more natural light.

Design: Marcia Miller and Steven Stein / Miller Stein Interior Design
Photography: www.davidduncanlivingston.com

Twisted Trick

A small, twisted kitchen layout was simplified and expanded by removing a wall to a breakfast nook. The new space focuses on the terrace, lovely gardens, and new pool in the backyard.

BEFORE

An expanded kitchen includes seating for three at a central island, and a magnificent range hood and display wall that create attractive interior elements.

◈ Warm wood tones are a marked departure from the stark black-and-white kitchen of before.

◈ Bronze accents are repeated in the lighting fixtures, countertop ledge brackets, and the cabinet pulls.

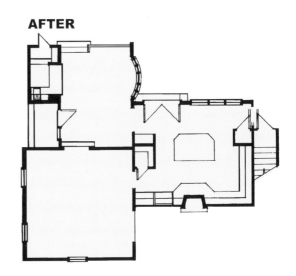

AFTER

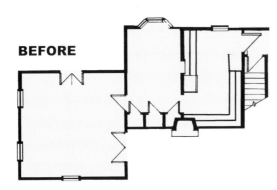

BEFORE

Jeannie & Alex Krumdieck / Krumdieck A+I Design, Inc.
Photography: Bob Gathany

Laundry Day

To increase the size of an existing kitchen, the wall between it and a laundry room was removed, along with a large, built-in closet. On the other side, a dining room wall was replaced with a 40 1/2" wall with a sill-cap for division. The laundry room is still functional, with an under-counter washer and dryer.

BEFORE

Granite countertops circle and connect this newly expanded kitchen. Stylish touches, including faux painting on the exposed beam and a pendant lamp add interest.

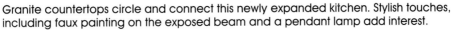

◈ Black crown moulding about the wall cabinets creates the illusion of greater height, and also parallels the sleek black counter.

◈ Diagonally placed tiling on the backsplash also helps to expand the space visually.

Design: Patricia Coats / Kitchens by Design of Sarasota
Photography: Lionel Murphy

Backyard Bliss

Owners of a mid-1970s home wanted to enhance the view of their attractive backyard. By adding on to their original kitchen they lightened up the originally dark space, and included a dining area that better reflected their lifestyle.

BEFORE

BEFORE

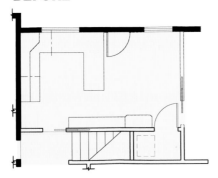

AFTER

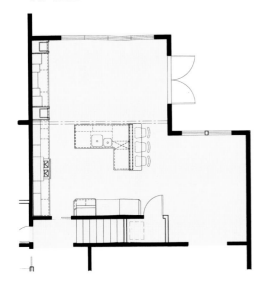

Deep red walls and oak hardwood floors envelop the room in warmth. Contrasting white trim draws attention to the large windows, which frame the gorgeous view of the backyard.

◈ A 219 square foot addition was built onto the back of the existing kitchen area. A bank of Pella windows and double French doors were included to flood the room with natural light and open up the view to the backyard.

◈ Customized Shaker-style cherry cabinets with a warm cinnamon stain were installed. A bank of cabinets with varied heights and depths, open shelves, and glass fronts flows from the kitchen to the dining area.

◈ Lighting was changed from an unattractive and impractical fluorescent fixture to ceiling cans and under-cabinet task lighting.

◈ Slab granite countertops in Tunis Green and stainless steel appliances were a welcome change from the outdated and mismatching originals.

Far left & Left:
The bank of cabinets provides form and function to the dining area by providing extra storage space and lighted glass-front display cabinets. Customized cabinets come stocked with storage options, including full-extension drawer guides, deep drawers, roll-shelves, a knife insert, and recycling bins.

Design: Marie A. Thompson, CKD, CBD / Showplace Design & Remodeling, Inc.
Photography: Roger Turk / Northlight Photography, Inc.

Eclectic Approach

A 1940s home was completely renovated. Replacing the existing sun porch and garage with the new kitchen, the homeowner wanted to preserve as much of the original home as possible. The goal was to create an eclectic, clean-looking, Georgian-styled space with lots of windows to maintain exterior views of the home's original gardens. Starting with a 150-year-old copper kettle and a green glass rolling pin the homeowner found in a Parisian flea market, the architects and designers created a fresh look in the new kitchen.

BEFORE

Copper accents, a variety of textures, and the combination of antique and contemporary French accessories lend a fresh look to this kitchen.

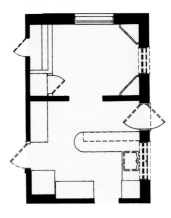

AFTER

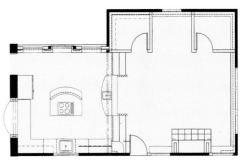

Glass "seeded" front cabinets and open shelves contribute to the kitchen's airiness. The custom window above the sink extends to the countertop for expanded outdoor views.

◈ Large windows were included in the new design to allow views of the gardens, built by the home's original owner, a landscape architect.

◈ Granite and copper countertops were installed, contributing to the eclectic look of the space. The copper farmer sink was custom made.

◈ The homeowner wanted two dishwashers for catering, and in order to get a "clean" look, all the stainless steel appliances were installed beneath the work surface. A traditional wall oven was excluded from the new design.

◈ Green was used to paint the hearth to match the custom brick wall and green glass rolling pin.

An arched cutout in the kitchen wall looks into the adjacent dining room, allowing the cook to remain in contact with guests and flooding the room with extra light.

Design: Christi Johaningmeyer / Architextures
Photography: David Kreutz & Associates

Peninsular Block

A U-shaped peninsula dominated the existing kitchen, blocking off the workspace from the rest of the room and directing incoming traffic through the cook's command center. Though the room had good bones, with a vast expanse of large windows and a tall cathedral ceiling, the owners wanted better amenities and a more efficient design in their kitchen. The new and improved design featured custom cabinetry with more storage in the cooking area, a thin pull-out pantry for spices, oil, and canned goods next to the refrigerator, a wet bar for entertaining, and an entertainment area with a desk. The results were dramatic, breathing fresh life into the originally stale space.

BEFORE

Sunny yellow walls, track lighting fixtures, and a gorgeous stone mantle add style to this kitchen. Quaker door style cabinets in hard maple are contrasted by darker mouldings. Sapphire blue granite countertops and backsplashes add more color to the kitchen and make for easy clean-up.

The Sub-Zero refrigerator without freezer and microwave/oven combination were chosen to save space. The microwave, which is convection, doubles as a second oven.

◈ The existing U-shaped peninsula was exchanged for a central island open on both sides. This reduced traffic through the workspace and created a much more open layout. A sink was placed in the island so the owner could enjoy the beautiful view from the large expanse of windows.

◈ To reduce the number of appliances and save space for other amenities, a microwave/oven combination and refrigerator-only unit were installed. The owners had a deep freeze in the adjacent mudroom, eliminating the need for one in the kitchen.

◈ A stone and wood mantle was constructed on the wall with the stovetop, creating a focal point in the tall room.

AFTER

The owners, who entertain frequently, wanted a wet bar included in their new kitchen design. A small refrigerator, icemaker, sink, and display cabinets for glassware provide a drink station for guests while the cook makes last minute preparations for parties.

Courtesy of Plain & Fancy Custom Cabinetry
Design: Morgan House Interiors
Photography: Simone Associates, Lebanon, PA

Room for Improvement

A couple that enjoyed cooking together and spent a lot of time in their home's kitchen found the room too tight and cramped to comfortably accommodate their needs. Outdated appliances and an awkward layout detracted from the joy of cooking, until the couple decided to build an addition onto their home and give their kitchen a complete makeover. Sleek and spacious, the remodeled kitchen was a drastic change.

BEFORE

BEFORE

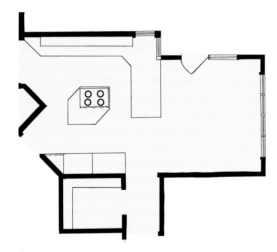

AFTER

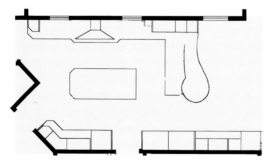

◈ An addition added space that the original kitchen lacked, giving the homeowners more options for laying out the new room.

◈ Designed for two cooks, the new kitchen features a main prep area around the sink, range, and peninsula, and a second cook area located at the island with ovens, steamer, and refrigerator.

◈ Recessed lighting and dramatic light fixtures were installed into the heightened ceiling, which added vertical height to the kitchen.

◈ Further drama was created in the kitchen with Birdseye maple cabinetry, glossy black granite countertops and accents, and tiled granite flooring.

Opposite page:
The range area was designed to be the focal area of the kitchen with fly-over piercing windows and a range hood hanging from the fly-over. Hand-painted tiles of the client's favorite wines were incorporated into the cooktop's backsplash.

Design: Cherie Brown / Kitchens By Kleweno
Photography: Steve Sanders

Diamond-Cut Addition

An addition expanded a home dramatically, creating a new kitchen area and a master bedroom. A five-sided bump-out on the addition created a picturesque breakfast nook, with a wall of light defining the new dining area. A lightened color scheme for the new cabinetry welcomed that light deep into the interior of the home.

Rich layers of moulding characterize the sunroom-like breakfast nook, and amplify the raised ceiling and second tier of windows. The enormous island serves up an abundance of surface for eating, food prep, and the cooktop.

BEFORE

◇ Large terracotta tiles unify kitchen and dining areas.

◇ The wide grid-work in the windows is consistent in both the breakfast nook and on the glass-fronted kitchen cabinets.

◇ Panels that match the cabinetry conceal the dishwasher, refrigerator, and trash compactor.

BEFORE   **AFTER**

Design: Peter Eckert / Architects' Guild
Photography: Olson Photographic, LLC

Family Command Center

A huge entertainment center once dominated the middle of this room. Removing it opened up space to create a great room/kitchen combination that more accurately reflected the lifestyle of a family that frequently entertains and always has a few children around – their own and others. A half-round floating counter has swivel bar stools that accommodate all five family members and allow them to watch TV while they eat. The banco style seating area was designed with kids in mind. The bottom of the seating area opens up to house all the on-going craft projects for the kids. The table was designed to work as one big family table or two kid project tables.

A bright and cheerful blue unifies living, dining, and food prep areas, and coordinates perfectly with an abundance of Arizona sky as viewed through windows and skylight.

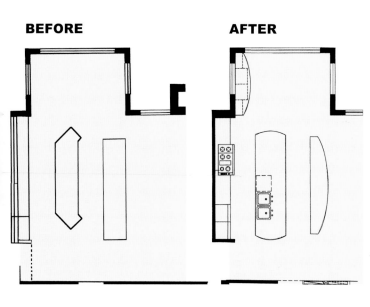

BEFORE

AFTER

◈ The countertops are a combination of rare granite Blue Macauba. For a different approach to the standard finished edges of stone, some of the counter edges were banded in stainless steel and copper. The half-round floating counter is a stainless steel top on wood legs.

◈ The ceiling was opened with a giant skylight, complete with electronic moving sun screen panels that regulate the sun from inside. Beaded valances are a finishing detail for windows that allow an unobstructed view of the Arizona mountains and a lush backyard.

Design: Lisa L. Reeves / Talents Design Studio
Photography: William Lesch

Classic Country Blues

Though they enjoyed a large expanse of space, these homeowners lacked storage in their kitchen. New cabinetry and a large island solved the problem. A new backsplash for the wonderful brick-enclosed range highlighted the space, and incorporated more storage. The room got a major update with the removal of fake beams and the creation of a new ceiling and lighting system. The old wood floors were repaired and refinished to complete this kitchen's transformation from a style-lacking yawner to a clean and classic country retreat.

◈ A "portable" island, set on castors with locks, replaced the original island, which was too large and awkwardly placed.

◈ Another island was installed to separate kitchen from family room, and includes a counter where the children can snack.

BEFORE

AFTER

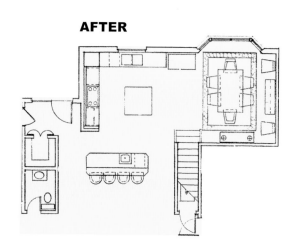

An antiqued Wedgewood blue finish on the butcher block island adds a keynote
of color to the room, echoed in the Willoware collection displayed over the range.

Design: Cheryl A. Van Duyne, ASID
Photography: Ira Montgomery, Dallas, TX

Going with the Flow

These homeowners wanted to open up their kitchen and family room to improve the flow of the house. They also requested more windows and French doors, with lots of area and task lighting to lighten up the kitchen. Narrow work isles and insufficient counter prep areas and storage options were also among the clients' laundry list of complaints about their original kitchen. A roomier kitchen, light colored cabinets chosen to blend with the contemporary country look of the house, and modern appliances made for an inviting and casual, yet elegant, makeover.

Hand glazed Santa Fe tiles in a soft, neutral color are used throughout the kitchen. A warm yellow was chosen to punctuate certain walls in the kitchen, dining, living, and family rooms to add brightness and give a sunny look to the space.

BEFORE

Natural alder cabinetry with mission style doors was softened with a "pillow" raised panel and satin finish.

◈ Return walls at the existing double oven, refrigerator, and island were removed. Walls into the dining room were opened by moving the hall closet and removing most of the southern wall. Thirty-four square feet from the deck area were incorporated to create generous work isles connecting various workstations.

◈ French doors were put in the existing breakfast area and a bow bay window was installed at the sink area, letting in ample light and allowing views of the garden.

◈ A large center island was included in the remodeled kitchen to provide extra workspace and seating. The muted terracotta and gray colored concrete island features a raised counter, warming drawer, and under counter refrigerator. The island's cabinetry was finished in a rich cabernet color to create a focal point and gathering space in the kitchen.

BEFORE   **AFTER**

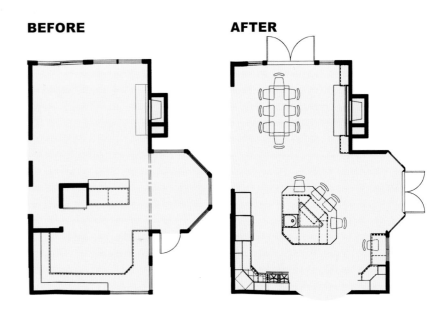

Design: Beverly Staal, CKD, CBD / Showplace Design & Remodeling, Inc.
Photography: Roger Turk / Northlight Photography, Inc.

Moving Out

BEFORE

A 1970s kitchen was badly in need of renovation. The owners wanted a simple, functional kitchen with clean lines and a style that better represented their lifestyle and taste. Everything from floor to ceiling was replaced to create a modern, fresh-looking space.

Clean lines and simple forms make the most of this kitchen's small space. Dark granite countertops and backsplash contrast beautifully with the ash cabinets.

◈ Ash cabinetry, stainless steel appliances, granite countertop and backsplash, and cherry floors are accessories hand-picked by the owners to reflect their needs and tastes.

◈ Glass-front cabinetry creates the illusion of more space while packing in the storage opportunities.

◈ An angled counter with a garden view was installed in the corner to provide a place for eating or prep work, making efficient use of the space.

◈ Large windows and a French door were included in the new design to open up the room by letting in more natural light.

Design: Marcy Voyevod Design
Contractor: David Adams

Cabinetmaker: Mueller Nicholls, Inc.
Photography: Muffy Kibby

Old World Redo

This 1970s home was renovated to capture the Old World atmosphere of permanence and quality. The kitchen area was reoriented to access a breakfast and keeping room beyond. To accommodate the owner's love of baking, dual islands and a wood-burning pizza oven were installed to allow everyone to participate in the activities.

Honeyed tones and classic design motifs lend an aura of Old World elegance.

BEFORE

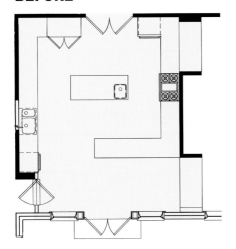

AFTER

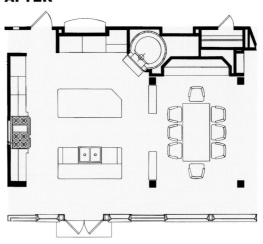

◈ Details include vaulted ceilings, timber beams, and rich wood details.

◈ Archways were introduced as openings between activity areas.

◈ Layers of materials were explored and include stained cypress, granite, stucco, tile, wood timbers, and reclaimed wood.

Design: Elizabeth Wilson & Alex Krumdieck / Krumdieck A+I Design, Inc.
Photography: Courtesy of Elizabeth Wilson

Infusing Warmth with Wood

Working in a limited space, these homeowners wanted all the amenities of a large kitchen, including a Viking Stove and Sub Zero refrigerator. Few changes were made to the original floorplan, making this kitchen an outstanding example of how minor changes can have a major effect in the appearance and function of a kitchen. Not the least among the changes was a color-theme makeover, ridding the room of the floor-to-ceiling white and installing glazed and stained maple cabinetry, walnut stained wide-plank hardwood floors, and Venetian gold granite countertops.

BEFORE

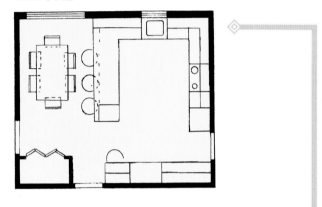

AFTER

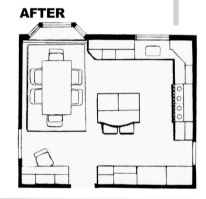

BEFORE

◈ Installing an island in place of a peninsula opened up the floor plan and changed the traffic flow and circulation of the space.

◈ A built-in pantry was replaced with a beautiful desk with ample drawers and a display hutch above.

Warm honeyed tones create an intimate atmosphere in this kitchen. The floor plan feels more open with the removal of a peninsula that created a backwater for traffic. The new layout allows flow all around an island and adjacent dining area.

Design: Diane Durocher, ASID
Photography: Jerry Kean

Rustic Woods

A cinderblock structure on a private lake was transformed to a new aesthetic, a rustic look that evoked a lived-in atmosphere, in tune with the natural beauty of the lake and woods surrounding the property. The space was gutted to create new ceiling heights and to relocate the plumbing. Salvaged oak was used for the interior partitions. A massive wood beam became a bar.

BEFORE

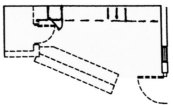

AFTER

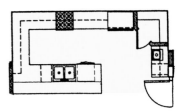

◈ Copper was used for the cypress cabinets, and a copper backsplash was cleverly incorporated to create the warm, lived-in atmosphere.

◈ Weathered, corrugated tin and tongue-and-groove decking were used on the ceilings.

◈ Concrete countertops were poured onsite to continue the no-polish rustic appearance.

Massive stretches of reclaimed lumber make this structure seem timeless. The rustic appeal is perfectly suited for the lakeside retreat.

Design: Jeannie & Alex Krumdieck / Krumdieck A+I Design, Inc.
Photography: Michael Neilson

Range Change

The owners of a newly purchased home wanted to improve the layout of their kitchen. A range on the center island limited the amount of prep area and gathering space available in the kitchen. Windows lining the walls posed a special design challenge by taking up valuable space. Here, windows were removed from the room in order to create a more efficient and sociable workspace.

BEFORE

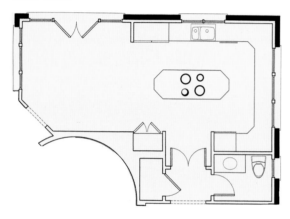

BEFORE

AFTER

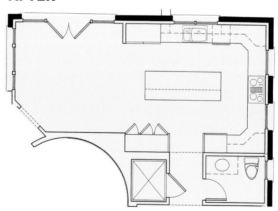

By moving the cook top to the wall area once occupied by a window, a focal point was created. A custom hood with carved accents complements the continuous soffit, which acts as decorative element and drapery pocket.

◇ Existing windows were replaced by larger ones, and the center window of the triple unit was removed.

◇ The cook top was moved from the center island to the area once occupied by the window.

◇ A new island was installed, offering bar seating and more workspace.

◇ All new custom wood cabinets, granite countertops, farmhouse style sink, and appliances were included in the design.

Design: Harrison Design Associates
Design Galleria Kitchen & Bath Studio

Limited Resources

A very cramped little kitchen had to expand, and the first and easiest solution was to appropriate an adjacent mudroom. The mere removal of the wall allowed a giant breath of fresh space into the room. Though also small, the mudroom allowed for a built-in seat and table to serve as a breakfast nook, and a natural attraction for removing anyone not actively engaged in food preparation. Within the kitchen, every ounce of wall was put to use to house storage and countertop workspace, with the exception of a very important double window over the sink. Storage also moved to a new pantry tucked between food prep areas and the nook.

The gray, green, and black of the granite countertops is repeated in the tile backsplash. The granite's tones work to unify the slick stainless steel appliances with the warm wood tones of the cabinetry.

BEFORE

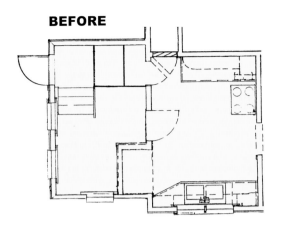

AFTER

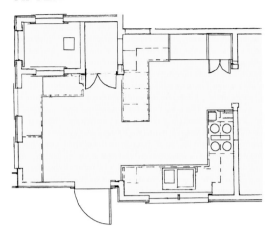

◈ The mud room's wall was removed to create more space in the kitchen.

◈ Arts and crafts styling is used consistently in the cabinetry, the decorative wood floor motif, and the leaded-glass cabinet door.

Design: Debbi Jacobs and Peter Eckert / Architects' Guild
Photography: Olson Photographic, LLC

59

Into the Light

Dark cabinetry, dark paint and wallpaper, and one small window begged to be remedied, and the designer reached out and engulfed a screened porch for an awe-inspiring solution. The resulting kitchen is nearly twice its former size, and the family has been happily herded out into the sunshine. A former breakfast nook was enclosed and transformed into an enviable pantry, while the open interior of the kitchen and dining area were enhanced with fine woodworking details that lend an aura of Old World elegance to the new surroundings.

By inserting an island in a different wood finish and granite countertop, the designer has created the effect of timeless furnishings.

BEFORE   **AFTER**

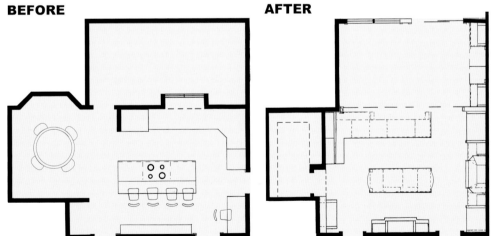

◈ To raise the ceiling, the drywall was removed, the ceiling joists were wrapped in cabinet-finish wood, and bead board was installed close to the decking above.

◈ A prep area for a second cook was set up on an island with a sink and refrigerator doors.

Design: Cherie Brown / Kitchens By Kleweno
Photography: Bob Greenspan

Distinctive Design

Homes set in residential developments usually feature distinct façades that differentiate one from another. The interior plans, however, are usually identical, as homeowners are normally required to work with the builder's choice of cabinetmakers and suppliers. The owners of a home in a New Jersey development knew that their kitchen looked like everybody else's in the neighborhood and wanted a design that set their kitchen apart from the rest. While the kitchen had good bones—attractive cabinetry, appliances, and wooden floors—a few structural and cosmetic changes gave the room a unique character.

BEFORE

◇ The ceiling was replaced by a three-tiered step design to add drama and elegance to the original kitchen.

◇ Further interest was created in the kitchen by removing the original stove hood and white tile backsplash, replaced by a sleeker-looking hood against a granite backsplash.

◇ The lighting plan was revised to accommodate the new ceiling and brighten previously dark spots in the kitchen.

◇ A new island was designed to accommodate the microwave, cookbook library, and more counter seating, thus freeing up more counter space.

BEFORE

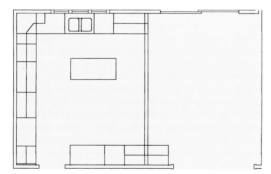

AFTER

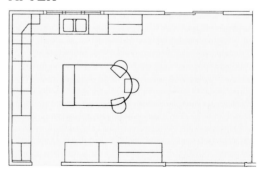

The ceiling's three-tiered step design gives this kitchen a completely different feel. A new
stove hood and granite backsplash that stretches to the ceiling accentuates the new design.

Design: Karla Trincanello, A.M. ASID / Interior Decisions, Inc.
Photography: Marisa Pellegrini

Penthouse Appointments

Commissioned by a client confined to a high-rise apartment, these designers had a long list of wishes to fulfill. A confining, dead-end kitchen was to be opened to the rest of the entertaining areas in the home, made larger to increase storage and counter space, include an eating area and bar, and to incorporate all of the modern conveniences while concealing them behind a nostalgic, furniture-like façade.

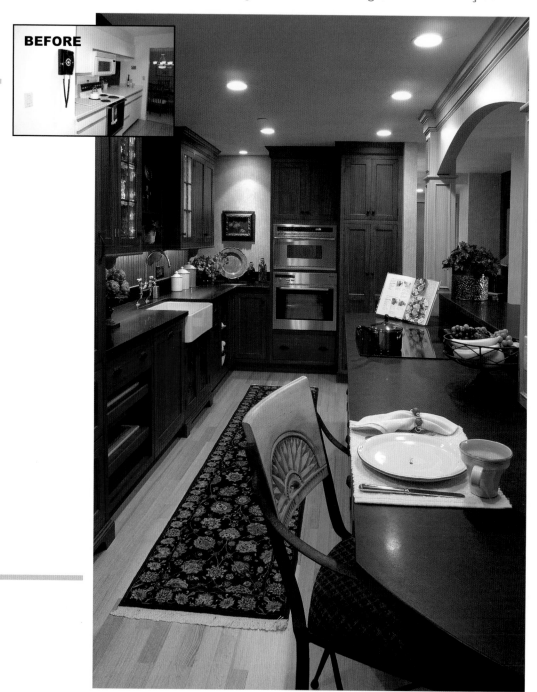

BEFORE

A hand-painted wall mural depicts a fabulous scene from the client's favorite Italian village, inviting visitors to the back of the kitchen, where island seating affords them a piece of the action, the host the pleasure of their company.

Design: Anne M. Fawcett, Allied ASID / Interiors by Decorating Den™
Cameron M. Snyder, CKD / Kitchen Concepts, Inc.

Wall Mural: Nancy Erving
Photography: John Ferrarone

BEFORE

Because he likes to entertain, this high-rise apartment owner placed priority on a bar in his gathering area. A working fireplace was also created to form a focal point for the room, and the view beyond was framed, a table placed there to invite passage toward the light.

BEFORE

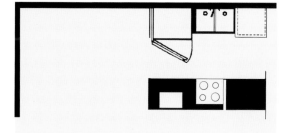

AFTER

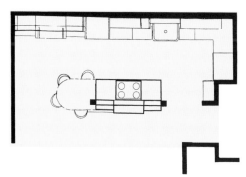

◈ The overall space and counters were increased by closing the original entryway, taking space from the hall, and eliminating the walls between the kitchen and former dining room.

◈ An apron sink, vintage faucet, custom tin panels, rollout baskets, and hardware were chosen to create a nostalgic look.

◈ Modern appliances including a Subzero 700 Series refrigeration system, a fully integrated dishwasher, warming drawer, cooking range, and even the ventilation system all but disappear behind wooden facades.

Sticking to the Plan

In this kitchen, a floorplan was left unaltered – the laundry room, the sitting and dining areas all left intact. In fact, the only physical modifications to the space involved cutting away the doorway that opened to the laundry area. But what a radical transformation. The central island was given a sleek new look, and cleared of its former cooking responsibilities. Instead, the range moved against the far wall, next to the sink, and the wall oven opposite the refrigerator. This allowed the island to become a central work and, most importantly, social station – the true heart of the kitchen.

◈ A high-style range hood and glass doors create a focal point on the back wall.

◈ Custom-designed bar stools and a stainless steel rail coordinate with the contemporary appliances and lighting.

◈ A wrap-around counter clears the old doorway area into the laundry, creating work and prep space both for kitchen and clothing chores. Also, a desk area was created in the laundry to utilize an otherwise wasted space.

BEFORE   **AFTER**

Design: Cherie Brown / Kitchens By Kleweno
Photography: Steve Sanders

The Power of Paint

The stark contrast of the smoky walls and white cabinetry simply didn't work, and this five-year-old kitchen was screaming for a fix. It was accomplished with a few simple steps – the cabinets were aged using a faux painting technique, and the walls were warmed up with a much lighter faux treatment. The large island was redesigned to encompass a larger countertop and a bead board pedestal with a crackle finish. Granite countertops were chosen to complement the overall scene. The previously teal support columns were finished a creamy off-white to create a more classic look.

Honeyed tones harmonize in this redesigned kitchen. A fantastic still-life dominates the breakfast area wall, a fitting focal point in a spacious room.

◇ Woven leather barstools and Windsor chairs around the dining area are handsome complements to the clean-lined, rustic atmosphere of the kitchen.

◇ The earthy tones of walls and furnishings work with the room's amenities – great wooden beams and random-width wood flooring.

Design: Jan Kyle Design
Photographer: José Santa Cruz

Spacious Sensation

A 1920s bungalow hadn't been updated since the 1950s – a remodel that left the kitchen complete with pink appliances and countertops atop maple cabinetry. Working with large, Marmoleum® squares, the designer adapted a pattern from Mexico, laying them on the diagonal to follow the angle of the peninsula. The overall effect is one of expanded space in the small kitchen. The kitchen also grew from its original footprint to encompass an unheated storage area that was expanded to encompass an open yet concealed pantry, a desk, and a small breakfast nook.

BEFORE

◈ The undercabinets are new, the wall cabinets are originals that were rescued from the basement and restored.

◈ The designer worked with the sunny yellow hues of Mexico, as well as a collection of provincial pottery to help establish her palette.

◈ The ceiling is a paintable wallpaper in a tile pattern.

Floor to ceiling doors and windows add light and an illusion of space to a small kitchen. A diagonal floor pattern, crafted from 20-inch Marmoleum® tiles, adds to the spacious effect, and creates a comfortable, foot-friendly surface.

Design: Judi Larkin / Lark Interiors
Photography: JDN Photography, Inc.
Architect: Donna Deasey

BEFORE

AFTER

Deco Re-do

BEFORE

In a truly startling renovation, an outdated kitchen was transformed into an Art Deco-inspired hangout. The owners wanted to recreate the style of the 1922 building, echoed in the new checkerboard floor tiles, absolute black granite countertops and white painted custom cabinetry, and in a tiled window surround that accentuates the precious sunlight afforded to this city apartment in San Francisco. The client's desire to dance with her husband in the evening inspired the designer to include strip lighting above the kickboard. Working within the confines of a multilevel concrete and steel structure, the designer managed to create a more functional and attractive space.

Stainless steel appliances house the latest technology in an apartment kitchen re-designed to echo its Art Deco heritage.

BEFORE

AFTER

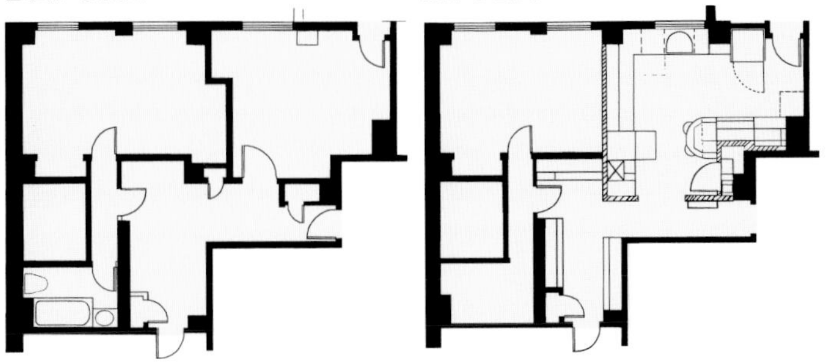

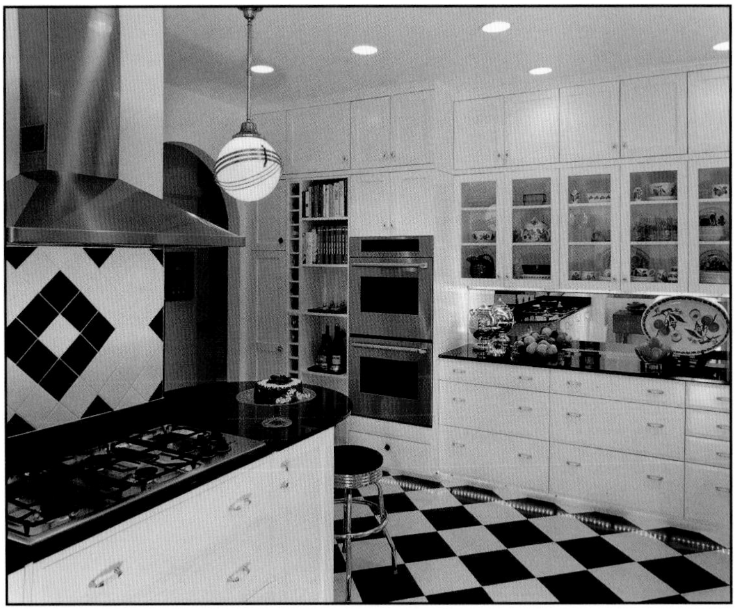

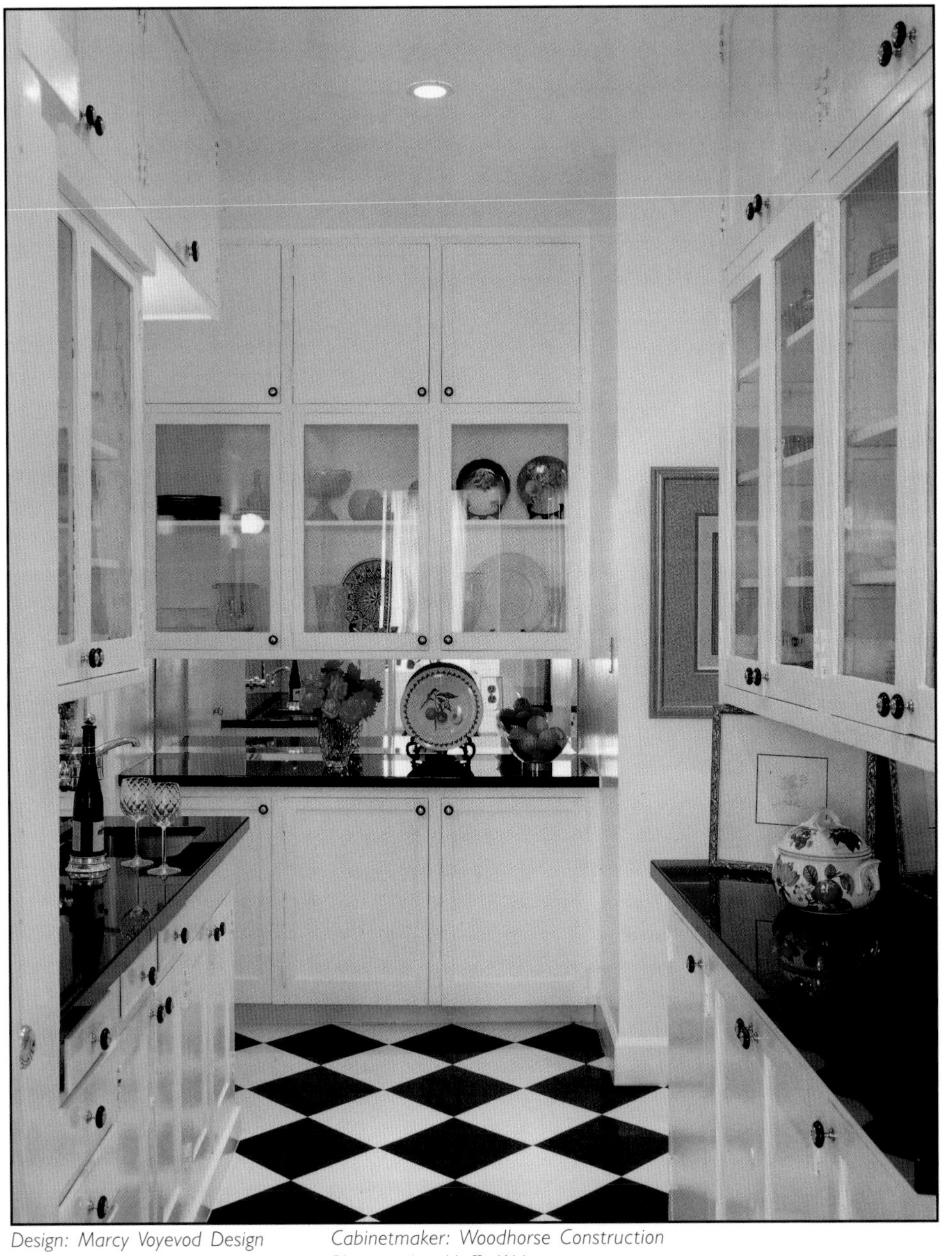

◈ Space was borrowed from an adjacent guest room.

◈ Extraneous closets and small doorways were removed in one corner of the kitchen to produce an open and graceful entry.

◈ An extended counter creates a dining area, eliminating the need for a kitchen table.

◈ The deco pendant lighting was a treasure, unearthed by the owner at an antique fair.

A butler's pantry serves as one entryway from the dining room to the kitchen, and the inclusion of a wet bar makes it a popular stop en-route when the couple entertains.

Design: Marcy Voyevod Design
Contractor: Murphy Construction
Cabinetmaker: Woodhorse Construction
Photography: Muffy Kibby

The Patio Problem

One of the biggest challenges faced by the designers of this project was how to deal with a 1970s remodel that filled in the patio outside the dining room and created a small courtyard off the kitchen. On top of this, the existing kitchen was oddly shaped, with a peninsula that jutted out into the center of the room. With a few changes in the kitchen's structure and layout, the architects managed to create a space that felt twice as big as the original.

Some of the features of this kitchen include French limestone countertops, Newport brass plumbing fixtures, a small window in the stovetop's backsplash, vintage lights from a Kentucky schoolhouse, and oil-rubbed bronze cabinet hardware.

BEFORE

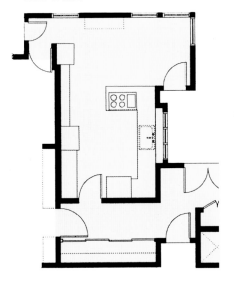

AFTER

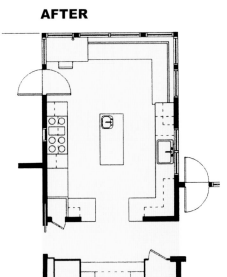

◈ The kitchen wall that bordered the original courtyard was pushed out several feet to meet the wall of the breakfast nook, thus adding lots of square footage to the room.

◈ More space was added to the kitchen by moving the range from a peninsula to the wall opposite the sink, and by replacing the peninsula with an island.

◈ A butler's pantry, complete with wine storage and a utility closet, was built in the place of the original laundry closet.

◈ Large windows were installed all along the breakfast room's walls to let in loads of light.

Design: Chris Barrett Design, Inc.
Architecture: KAA Design Group
Photography: Tim Street Porter

Family Oriented

The owners of this kitchen wanted to create a more usable family area in the kitchen, without losing functional cooking and eating space. They also requested access to the backyard from the kitchen and a design that took advantage of the kitchen's panoramic views of Lake Washington, without intruding on other living spaces or impeding the original flow of the kitchen.

The new design incorporated a traditional style cabinet to blend with the home's original architecture. A combination of brass and stainless steel hardware was used to incorporate the new stainless steel appliances.

By adding 34 square feet with a bay, the designers fulfilled their clients' wishes to take advantage of the stunning view and create a space with a warm, family atmosphere. The larger and brighter eating area, complete with an upholstered chair, provides a desirable gathering space for family members.

BEFORE

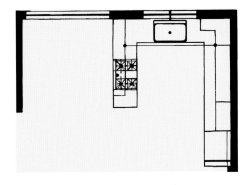

◈ The kitchen was stripped to the studs. A bay window and a door with steps to the existing deck were added with 34 extra square feet.

◈ Instead of a peninsula, an island was included in the kitchen's new design to maximize efficiency of the workspace.

◈ Wood floors were extended from the rest of the house into the room.

AFTER

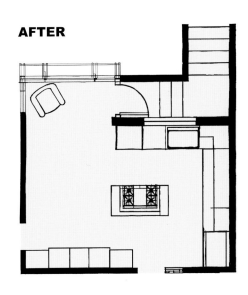

Design: Torrell Architects
Photography: R. Lauris Bitners

Time Warp

The existing kitchen was small and dark, with inadequate storage space but a large breakfast area. Some structural adjustments to the room, a sleek, modern look, and brand new stainless steel appliances helped to breathe new life into the struggling kitchen and surrounding spaces.

White walls, light-colored cabinetry, and stainless steel appliances amplify the amount of light in the kitchen.

◈ The first step was to seal the back door, which added several extra feet of wall space.

◈ The wall and cabinets at the cook top were pushed back 5' into the living room to enlarge the workspace.

◈ A free hanging hood was installed to keep the small kitchen open to the adjacent living room – adding space and light to the area.

◈ Surface materials from the rest of the house were also used in the kitchen to create the illusion of a larger, continual space.

BEFORE   **AFTER**

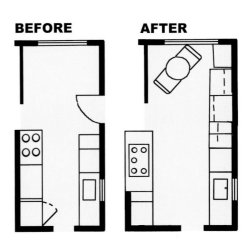

Design: Umphrey Interiors
Photography: Michael Gary Owen

Extended Change

The original objectives for this remodeling project were to create a kitchen large enough and with the appropriate amenities for two serious cooks, and create a somewhat formalized dining room area that was separate from the living room. An addition was built, creating a wing that extended from the front of the house, almost doubling the size of the kitchen and making room for a larger dining room.

The original load-bearing wall of the kitchen was painted a deep blue and given an off-white wash for a more antique look. Hickory was chosen for the cabinetry, as was practically indestructible lab top material for the counters flanking the stove and the backsplash.

BEFORE

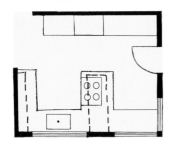

AFTER

◈ The entire kitchen was gutted except for the load-bearing wall, which separated it from the master bedroom.

◈ Eight feet of the original deck were reclaimed by the interior of the home.

◈ The original load-bearing wall contained older built-in cabinetry, a wall oven, and the refrigerator. The wall oven was kept as a second oven, open shelves were fitted into the refrigerator space, and the remaining cupboards were retrofitted with sliding pullout shelving. A new utility closet was also fitted into this wall.

Design: Torrell Architects
Photography: R. Lauris Bitners

Warming Up

An infusion of warm tones enlivened this kitchen, creating a dynamic new space in the same basic footprint as the previous kitchen. A multi-color tile backsplash tops the new sleek black countertop, and warm wood tones in the cabinetry add mellow contrast to the new cork floor.

BEFORE

Repeating squares in the tiles, chairbacks, and even framed art over the dining table lend a warm motif to the new environment.

BEFORE

AFTER

◇ The refrigerator and range traded spaces in the floorplan.

◇ A larger dining space was created by eliminating a loveseat in the activity area in exchange for two comfy chairs.

Design: Joseph Hittinger Designs
Photography: Ken Rice

Historic Re-creation

The kitchen in an 1896 house had been gutted before the new owners purchased it, so there were no original clues to work from but a wonderful blank space filled with light. After a lot of research on the period, the owners embraced the idea of restoring the entire house to what it might have looked like in 1896, while ensuring that it had modern conveniences such as a paraprofessional Viking stove. Using an architectural device common in homes of the period, the designers created a low wall with columns flanking the passageway between the kitchen and dining room.

Cherry cabinetry lends warm antique tones to this room. In the center, a custom maple-topped cabinet with glass-front bin drawers on both sides anchors the arrangement.

BEFORE

BEFORE

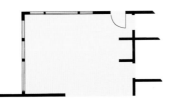

AFTER

 A custom hammered copper hood caps the range area, and copper-framed art glass panels combining new and antique glass were used for display cabinets.

◈ Green granite was selected for its durability as countertop material.

◈ The backsplashes are simple, white, 3"x 6" tiles, typical of the time period.

Design: Marcia Miller and Steven Stein / Miller Stein Interior Design
Photography: www.davidduncanlivingston.com

Saving Space

Limited lighting was this homeowner's major concern. She wanted the kitchen to better reflect the style of the rest of the house by incorporating the color palette of the dining and living rooms, and allowing it to blend with her collection of Victorian furnishings. Without any major structural changes, the outdated kitchen was modernized while maintaining a Victorian ambience.

Three different countertops were used in the kitchen to add visual interest. A cream colored Formica edged in cherry wood was used near the sink area, the island was topped with a green marble, and the counter on the breakfront was cherry.

BEFORE

BEFORE

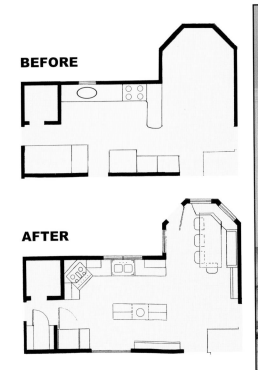

AFTER

A custom green mosaic inset in the floor beneath the kitchen table and a green painted breakfront complement the island's green marble countertop.

◈ The opening to the dining room was enlarged and a peninsula that jutted out into the middle of the kitchen was removed.

◈ Adding hardwood floors linked the living and dining rooms with the kitchen, making the area seem larger.

◈ Placing the refrigerator where the washer and dryer had been opened up the corridor to the family room.

◈ To let in more light, the only window in the kitchen area was enlarged and moved closer to the room's main area. Stationary sidelights were added to the dining room's opening to let light filter into the kitchen.

Design: Joan Nemirow Designs, LLC
Photography: David Todd Photography

Narrow Margin of Error

A long and narrow kitchen was badly in need of a makeover. Big cabinets hanging above the peninsula cut the room in two, making it feel much smaller. The combination of tile and carpet flooring, and a large brick fireplace in the center of the room also had a shrinking effect on the space. The designer's main goals were to update the kitchen and create a more inviting atmosphere there.

BEFORE

BEFORE

AFTER

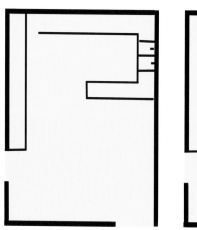
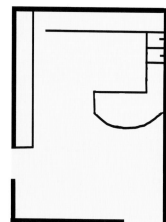

◇ The quartz counter against the wall with a window was lengthened by two feet to create a larger prep area, and cabinets hanging above the peninsula were removed.

◇ The addition of a half circle peninsula added extra seating and gave width to the room.

◇ Installing exotic wood flooring throughout the kitchen and adjacent family room area unified the space and gave the impression of a roomier layout.

The designer chose natural maple cabinets to blend with the wood flooring. A dark chocolate brown quartz countertop provides contrast to the lighter cabinetry and flooring.

Design: Angela Morton Interior Design
Photography: Nicholas Nawroth

Out of Place

Surrounded by undeveloped woodland acreage, a kitchen with a style dubbed "Retro Jet 707" by a friend of the owners,' was out of place in their country classic home. Grey vinyl-clad cabinets, grey floor tiles, and dark wallpaper formed a look that was dark and inappropriate in the otherwise light, warm, and airy home. Even their realtor, who had built and lived in the house, apologized for the kitchen, saying, "I knew this was a mistake the minute the cabinets started to go up." In addition to its style faux pas, the kitchen's appliances were dated and inconveniently laid out, fluorescent lighting was inadequate, and available storage space did not meet the homeowners' needs. With a constrained budget and lots of creative planning, the kitchen was beautifully modified to reflect the style of the rest of the house while meeting the needs of the homeowners.

BEFORE

◈ To stay within a limited budget, the original space of the kitchen was maintained, keeping the existing placement of walls, windows, French doors to the deck, and other entries.

◈ The most notable change in the kitchen's layout was the repositioning of the double oven doors, which originally opened directly in front of the dining room's entry.

◈ Pristine white cabinetry with glass fronts was chosen to reflect natural light from the windows; and mouldings, ceiling, and walls were also painted white.

◈ The owners chose a custom farmhouse sink made from patterned stainless steel to add to the kitchen's contemporary country atmosphere. This same material was used in the stove's backsplash.

◈ Stunning granite was used for the countertops and backsplashes, adding texture and a focal point to the kitchen.

◈ Halogen and other white-light fixtures replaced fluorescent lighting.

AFTER

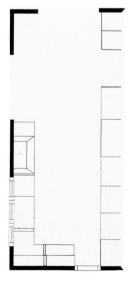

Oak flooring was installed in the renovated kitchen to unite the space with adjacent rooms in the house and to give it a warmer atmosphere.

"Azul Newport" granite features prominently in the renovated kitchen. The swirling blue, grey, and white pattern of the natural stone, with reflective mica and amber highlights remind the homeowners of the nearby ocean.

Design: Gaye Weatherly / Weatherly Tile & Stone, Inc.
Photography: ©2003 Jan D. Armor

An Epicurean's Dream

BEFORE

A former food stylist and dedicated epicurean felt limited by the confined, U-shaped configuration of his kitchen, which didn't permit the state of the art equipment and workspaces that he so coveted. A dark, cramped, and unexciting arena for the pursuit of a lifelong passion, the original kitchen sadly possessed inadequate storage, counter space, and lighting. Obsolete appliances and outmoded cabinetry made the homeowner even more desirous of a new venue where he could perform his favorite craft. The results were amazing, a truly wonderful combination ergonomic function and aesthetics.

Conscious of diminishing forest resources, the clients wanted to use laminate finishes on cabinetry balanced by natural finishes elsewhere. The cabinets were selected not only for a sleek, understated, flush panel door style, but also for formaldehyde free box construction. The balance of polished and matte surfaces creates textural interest.

The client requested storage for an enormous cookbook collection and space for a laptop computer, telephone, and mail, in addition to plenty of storage space for a wide array of utensils, appliances, spices, and cooking oils. The request was answered with the custom cabinetry and a cherry butcher-block topped desk.

◈ A wall was removed between the kitchen and an adjacent and seldomly used sitting area. Unifying the space doubled the kitchen size, while allowing the clients to fully enjoy a verdant hillside view.

◈ A large, teardrop shaped island was built with ample seating for three, fourteen feet of a buffet counter, dish storage with easy access to the cleanup area and eating nook, secondary recycling, storage for cutting boards, a prep sink with garbage disposal, oven, and wine cooler.

◈ Brushed stainless steel halogen commercial suspension lighting was customized to hang at a lower height, not only to provide lighting for the island prep area, but to warm plated food as well.

BEFORE

AFTER

Design: Diane Foreman, CKD / Showplace Design & Remodeling, Inc.
Photography: Roger Turk / Northlight Photography, Inc.

Ranch Dressing

A 1957 ranch was due to reorganize and expand. The kitchen was converted into a dining space and an exterior patio was used as the slab for an addition. Layers of materials were explored and included stained cypress doors and trim work reclaimed from a 1920s resort hotel. The trim was kept at eight feet to maintain an intimate scale in the newly elevated, ten-foot tall room. Finishes include a natural random plank cypress floor, ebony stained Shaker-style cabinets, and square-edged concrete countertops. Appliances were chosen in stainless steel, and contemporary yellow-orange glass pendant fixtures were selected to float over the island.

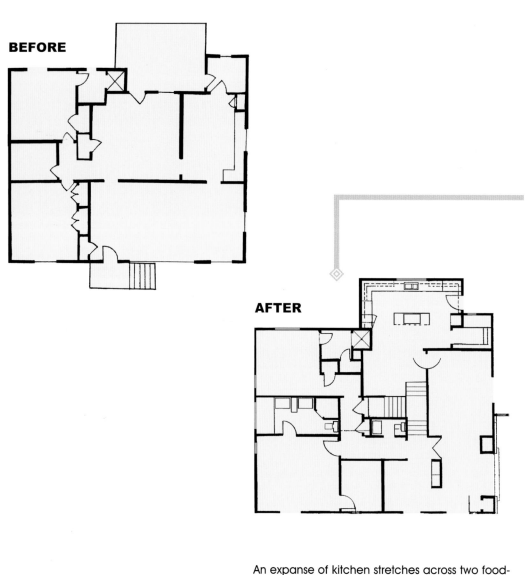

BEFORE

AFTER

An expanse of kitchen stretches across two food-prep islands to an outside wall banked by windows.

◈ An amber glass tile backsplash and sunflower yellow painted walls create a warm and unpretentious setting for family meals and entertaining.

BEFORE

Design: Jeannie & Alex Krumdieck / Krumdieck A+I Design, Inc.
Photography: Michael Neilson

Artful Transformation

In a light-filled seaside home, the original kitchen failed to function effectively as an efficient workspace and as an enjoyable center of the home. The small work area was mostly closed off from exterior views and adjoining areas, limiting traffic flow, and the space was badly in need of modernization.

BEFORE

AFTER

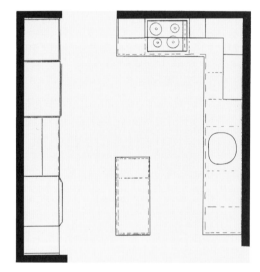

Clean lines and the combination of sleek and textured surfaces reflect the personalities of this kitchen's owners – relaxed, quietly elegant, and comfortably modern.

◇ Part of a wall was removed to expose stunning views of the backyard and gardens.

◇ A central island, with loads of drawers, was added to provide extra workspace without inhibiting the movement of the couple, who both contribute to the cooking duties of the household. The custom designed drawers were configured to hold just about anything.

◇ Maple cabinets and granite surfaces were installed to complement the gorgeous natural views that now hang as the permanent backdrop to the new kitchen.

Design: Gaye Weatherly / Weatherly Tile & Stone
Photography: Jan D. Armor

BATHS
Planning for the Future

A retired professional couple with grandchildren wanted a bathroom design that emphasized safety and function, natural light illumination, and elements that would blend with the existing architecture and a collection of Asian art. An addition was built onto the existing master bedroom to house the new bath, which was designed to be a garden lover's quiet retreat for pampering, relaxation, and a place to enjoy the sweeping hillside views.

BEFORE

Solid slab granite countertops and tub deck are complemented by vertical grain fir cabinets with a natural finish. Neutral tiles with a slight green tint create a geometric pattern around the room, which was painted in soft green to match. Mosaic tiles were used in the vanity backsplash and in the shower to create interest.

A large picture window was placed at the tub area to enable the owners to enjoy the gorgeous natural vies. Shoji screens were used to give privacy and to add to the room's Asian flair.

◈ Wide entries into the bathroom, the shower, and toilet areas, in addition to an open floorplan were designed for wheelchair accessibility.

◈ The shower floor is flush with the rest of the bathroom to meet accessibility requirements.

◈ Decorative grab bars were included in the shower, and all the walls in the bath were reinforced for more to be installed later if necessary.

AFTER

BEFORE

Design: Beverly Staal, CKD, CBD / Showplace Design & Remodeling, Inc.
Structural Design: Michele Marquardi and Lucia Pizzio / Ectypos
Photography: Roger Turk / Northlight Photography, Inc.

English Challenge

An outdated bath was updated to fit with the European flair found throughout the rest of the home. Two designers collaborated on the project after Rose Burcheri, who'd designed other rooms in the home, brought in Sherry Joyce of SJ Designs to collaborate on the master bath. Taking its cue from a curved dresser in the master bedroom, the cabinetry, counter, and fixtures were selected and cut to fit the oval theme. The 1 1/2-inch granite counters unify the room, from a vanity area at the entry, through to the oval soaking tub. Honey-toned limestone provides the footing, interspersed with black and burgundy glass tiles. The owner now claims this room as her sanctuary after a hectic day, and says that, with lit candles and aromatherapy, it becomes difficult to leave.

A new master got a facelift, from the floor to the lighting fixtures. All of the elements were an outgrowth of a theme lifted from a beautiful curved-front dresser found in the master bedroom beyond. Even the English damask floral chair continues the design of curving lines.

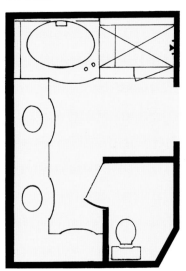

AFTER

◈ Arched mirrors continue the curvilinear theme, while providing the illusion of more space.

◈ Oval set-in sinks sit side-by-side, surrounded by a luxurious expanse of granite countertop with an ogee bevel edge.

Design: Sherry Joyce / SJ Designs
Rose Burcheri / Interiors by Decorating Den
Photography: Sherry Joyce / SJ Designs

Contemporary Solution

The original bathroom in a 1958 house had never been updated. Bright blue tile walls and busy wallpaper made the narrow space feel more confining, which was long overdue for a makeover.

◇ The vanity counter was replaced with an antique sideboard that was refinished and fitted for a sink. The doors were covered with brushed stainless steel sheets and finished with silver hardware.

◇ Existing crown moldings were removed to give the sense of more height.

◇ An oversized mirror was included in the design to visually expand the space. The stainless steel doors of the sideboard also have this effect.

The bathroom achieves a sleek, contemporary look with pale grey walls, black window trim, black tile flooring, and an antique sideboard finished with brushed stainless steel doors.

BEFORE

Design: Umphrey Interiors
Photography: Michael Gary Owen

Bungalow Bath

These homeowners wanted a brighter, larger-feeling bathroom with increased storage. As part of an extensive interior remodeling job, the bathroom's layout and structure were kept the same, but the style was updated to reflect the owners' tastes and a new decade.

AFTER

BEFORE

◈ The bathroom was tiled in slate wainscott to create an elegant look. The same tile was also used on a counter built above the commode and behind the sink.

◈ A large mirror occupying the entire wall behind the sink was hung to visually expand the tiny bathroom.

◈ A tall cabinet was constructed into the wall to provide extra storage.

Design: Torrell Architects
Photography: R. Lauris Bitners

A large mirror works wonders to make this tiny bathroom feel larger.

A Style that Grows

The tiny original bath was part of a 1960s remodel of a 1926 home. The owners decided that the entire second story of the home was in need of renovation, and it was pushed two feet to the rear. A new layout, more space, and décor chosen to age well with the children who would be using the bathroom produced dramatic results.

BEFORE

◈ With two more feet available to use in the bathroom's layout, the shower stall was changed to a larger tub and shower, and pushed up against the far wall. A small linen closet was put in the shower's original place.

◈ The commode was moved to the opposite wall, next to the newly installed double sinks that were included to more comfortably fulfill the needs of the owners' two children.

Yellow tile with an accenting multicolored geometric pattern is playful enough for the young users of the bath, yet sophisticated, too. This will suit their changing tastes as they mature into young adults.

Design: Marcia Miller and Steven Stein / Miller Stein Interior Design
Photography: www.davidduncanlivingston.com

Reconfigured

A master bath was drastically reconfigured to meet the needs of an aging client. To make the room more universally accessible, a tub made way for a roomy walk-in shower with a seat. A double-sink vanity area was reduced in size to create the appearance of more space in the room, and to lend access to a closet.

BEFORE   **AFTER**

◈ A pocket door replaced a folding door to increase the visual appeal of the master bath entrance and to overcome a conflict with the entry door from the hallway.

◈ Sliding doors were installed to replace a wall and folding door, making the back areas of the closet more accessible visually.

Wall sconces work with the honey tones of this master bath.

Design: Joseph Hittinger Designs
Photography: Ken Rice

Optical Illusions

A designer wanted to maximize space in her small bathroom, while adding Old World charm to blend with her large collection of French antiques. Old tile, cabinetry, and limited light also impelled the designer to remodel her bath, along with the desire to include a stall shower as well as a separate whirlpool tub. With some minor structural changes, a major reconfiguration to the bath's layout, and a few design tricks, the small space was completely transformed.

BEFORE

The designer and owner of this bath wanted to give it a 17th century French flair. Three different types of marble, period brass fittings, and an elaborate window treatment all work to this effect.

◈ The entire bath was gutted, and space was taken from the bathroom and hall linen closets to make room for a new stall shower.

◈ The original window was replaced by a larger, French window to allow in more light.

◈ To elongate the space and give the impression of more width, the whirlpool tub was placed horizontally against the far wall, and surrounded by custom cherry cabinetry.

◈ Mirrors were hung throughout the bath to amplify light and give the impression of space.

◈ The use of a custom pedestal sink visually enlarges the bath by opening up floor space.

BEFORE

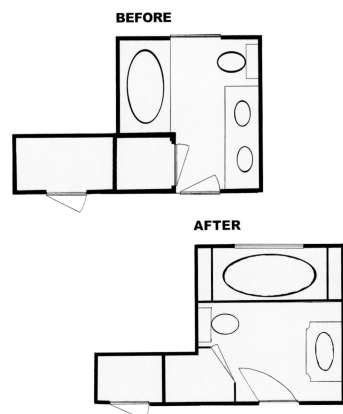

AFTER

Design: Joan Nemirow Designs, LLC
Photography: David Todd Photography

Split Decision

A bath by the foyer served as both master bath and make-shift guest bath. These homeowners found the entrance from the master bedroom into the bath inconvenient, and wanted a more updated look for the room. The space was reorganized to create an upscale master bath and separate powder room for a more practical and attractive configuration.

BEFORE

Custom cherry cabinetry, marble slab countertops, and marble tiles were used to create a magnificent look for this elegant bath, finished with an antiqued mirror chandelier and bamboo roman shades.

A richly decorated powder room has a strie glaze finish on the walls. The vanity was purchased in the south of France and the lighting is Italian.

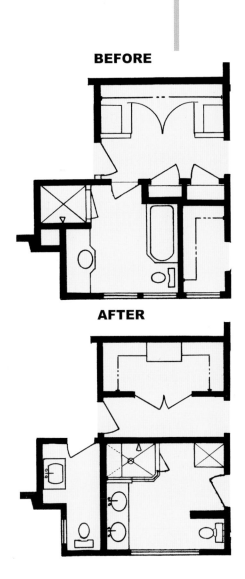

BEFORE

AFTER

◈ Walls between the original bathroom and various closets – including a master bedroom walk-in – were removed so that the new master bath would have a private entrance from the bedroom, and new space was allocated for a powder room.

◈ Two small windows were replaced by one large one in the master bath to allow more light and to create a more elegant look. A small window was added to the powder room as well.

◈ Built-in cabinetry was removed from a dressing area, and a wall was added to make a new walk-in closet in the master bedroom.

Design: Christian Huebner Interiors, Inc.
Photography: Mark Sinclair

Figured Out

A busy computer software executive and his wife felt cramped in their master bathroom. The tub area was too small to fit the tall couple, and inadequate storage, lighting, and ventilation accompanied by a narrow entry made the large bath seem confining. No space could be taken from the small, adjacent bedroom area, necessitating a reconfiguration that maximized limited resources for additional space. This, in combination with a dramatic choice in colors and materials that mirrored the home's lakeside setting produced dramatic results.

Gray-green slate and deep, dark green and gold speckled granite tiles with rough-hewn broken edges were used to tile the walls. The vanity mirror was laser cut to match the uneven, broken edges of the tiles, creating the impression of a pool of water. Countertop mounted mottled glass lavatory vessels look like carved rock crystals and add to the bath's sensation of being in a natural grotto.

BEFORE

A two person whirlpool tub and lighting switched to a computerized digital control pad provide the clients with luxury and control over lighting combinations to suit their varying moods and needs.

The designer consulted the taller than average clients to determine the most comfortable height of the showerheads and body sprays.

BEFORE

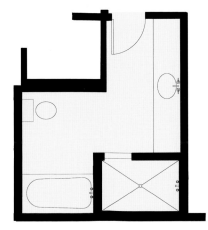

AFTER

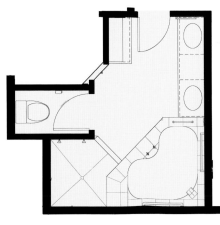

◈ Space was taken from one of two entry closets to create a compartment for the bath's commode. At the request of the client to relocate the laundry shoot within the master bath, space was taken from an adjacent powder room.

◈ A skylight was constructed and eight recessed can lights were installed. The addition of the skylight to the windowless room produced the impression of a bigger space.

◈ The taller than average heights of the clients were addressed by installing lavatory vessel sinks 37 1/2" above the finished floor, and installing fixtures at a comfortable height.

◈ A hydronic floor heating system linked to the existing water heater was installed to provide the bath with soothing warmth.

Design: Diane Foreman, CKD / Showplace Design & Remodeling, Inc.
Photography: Roger Turk / Northlight Photography, Inc.

Rehabbed Bath

BEFORE

A small, 100 year old Victorian had been internally destroyed during its tenure as a poorly maintained rental home. The cottage was in need of a major renovation – especially the first floor bathroom, which seemed like an architectural afterthought in its original place at the back of the house. The designer's goal was to enhance the original house's character, with its gingerbread, simple millwork, and Old World charm, while updating its floorplan to reflect the owners' lifestyle.

BEFORE

AFTER

◈ After gutting the original bathroom to make room for the dining room and a kitchen addition, a connecting foyer and new bathroom were created in the closet space between two bedrooms.

◈ A delicately styled Swedish commode with pull flush, tiled Japanese style soaking tub, and pedestal sink were installed.

Opposite page:
The original bathroom was placed at the rear of the house, with windows immodestly overlooking the back porch. Although the entire bath was gutted and moved elsewhere, the designer followed the Victorians' lead and installed white-painted groove paneling in the new bathroom to keep with the home's style. White and cobalt blue tile and white wainscot are marvelously paired with alabaster, ceramic, and chrome fixtures to create a space that is at once airy and intimate.

Design: Lisa Leigh Johnson Interior Design Studio

Blank State

Starting with a blank canvas, this powder room evolved from an antique vanity and
mirror that were paired with a modern basin and faucet for a striking blend of old and new.

◆ A ceiling pendant and wall sconces infuse the room with a
golden glow through honey tones of silk. A Venetian plaster
finish on the walls completes the sense of antiquity in the room.

BEFORE

AFTER

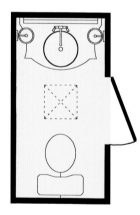

Bowl sinks have
become increasingly
popular, adding to
the desire for "furnish-
ings" in rooms as
opposed to stock
cabinetry.

Design: Donna Livingston / dl design inc.
Photography: Tripp Smith

Enter Exotica

Building on a black tiled floor and sink unit, the designer incorporated the exotic for this hygienic retreat. Black shutters and trim were added to the two windows to ensure privacy, and the color is repeated in the shower curtain, towels, and the zebra rug.

◈ A bamboo mirror is in keeping with the room's East/ Southeast orientation.

◈ A Regency-style bookcase with a black wax finish adds sophistication and polish.

Sepia-toned animal prints were matted and framed with similar hues, and hung to add illusion of space to the room.

BEFORE

Design: Patricia McLean Interiors, Inc.
Photographer: Robert Thein

Asian Update

A flowery guest bath underwent a drastic cosmetic makeover. Though the floorplan wasn't varied, the flowers were stripped away and new cabinetry was installed with countertop at two levels to help break up the expanse.

BEFORE

A wide "chair rail" of 1/2" tiles grounds the room, establishing a unifying stripe in a mid-tone between the rich earthen hues of cabinetry and countertops and the expanse of white above.

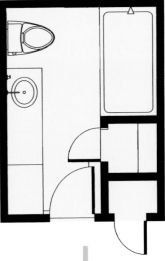

◈ An Asian effect is created with accessories – raku pottery, an artful flower arrangement, and wall art.

Design: Joseph Hittinger Designs
Photography: Bernardo Grijalva

Master Touch

The lady of the house wanted a much bigger tub for luxurious soaks, the gentleman preferred to stand and shower. Their demands necessitated a clever rethinking of the floorplan.

BEFORE

Wood tones add to the Zen-like atmosphere created for soothing, candlelit soaks in a wonderful new tub.

BEFORE

AFTER

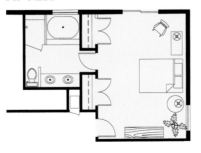

◈ A much larger tub becomes the central attraction in a redone bathroom. Once in, the new vanity – featuring fantastic, custom wood inlay work in a harlequin motif – offers up a stunning view.

◈ A walk-in closet was sacrificed to the hygienic needs of two masters of the house. In exchange, they got equal his and hers closets.

Design: Joseph Hittinger Designs
Photography: Bernardo Grijalva

Accommodating Guests

These homeowners wanted their full guest bath to double as powder room for guests who wouldn't be staying. Shutter bi-fold doors were used to conceal the tub when not in use, creating the illusion of a linen closet and accomplishing the two-zone objective. The rest was pure upgrade. A whirlpool tub replaced the shower stall; a custom vanity was created in exotic Lacewood and capped with limestone; crown, door, and ceiling mouldings added; and, finally, a decorative mural in soft neutrals was painted in both rooms.

BEFORE

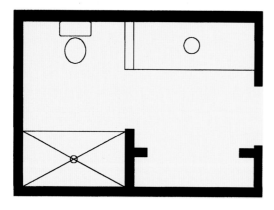

AFTER

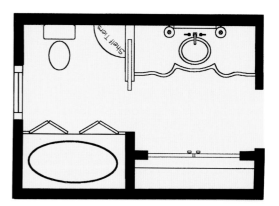

◈ Louvered panels in the doors that conceal the tub allow for ventilation after bathing.

◈ A mirror with electrified sconces creates a focal point on a mirrored wall.

Design: Karla Trincanello, A.M. ASID / Interior Decisions, Inc.
Photography: Marisa Pellegrini

Contributors

Angela Morton Interior Design
3665 Nantucket Dr. #F
Loveland, OH 45140
(513) 702-3000
www.angelamortoninteriordesign.com

Architects' Guild
137 Greenwood Ave.
Bethel, CT 06801
(203) 791-8778
www.architectsguild.net

Arichitextures
7905 Big Bend Boulevard
Saint Louis, MO 63119
314-961-9500
www.architexturesllc.com

Cheryl A. Van Duyne, ASID
14902 Preston Rd., Ste. 404-775
Dallas, TX 75254
(972) 387-3070
www.cherylvanduyne.com

Chris Barrett Design, Inc.
1640 19th St.
Santa Monica, CA 90404
(310) 586-0774
www.chrisbarrettdesign.com

Christian Huebner Interiors, Inc.
15 N. Ellsworth Ave., Ste. 100L
San Mateo, CA 94401
(650) 558-8700
www.huebnerinteriors.com

dl design inc.
229 S. Caswell Rd. ste. 2
Charlotte, NC 28204
(704) 377-7036
www.dldesigninc.com

Depew Design Interiors
248 Addie Roy Rd., Ste. B106
Austin, TX 78746
(512) 347-9876
www.depewdesign.com

Design 2 Interiors
90 Great Oaks Blvd., Ste. 103
San Jose, CA 95119
(408) 284-0100
www.design2interiors.com

Design Galleria Kitchen & Bath Studio
351 Peachtree Hills Ave. NE, Ste. 234
Atlanta, GA 30305
(404) 261-0111
www.designgalleria.net

Diane Durocher Interiors
375 South Central Ave.
Ramsey, NJ 07446
(201) 825-3832

Harrison Design Associates
3198 Cains Hill Place, NW, Ste. 200
Atlanta, GA 30305
(404) 365-7760
www.harrisondesignassociates.com

Inside Incorporated
2038 Ward Parkway
Fort Worth, TX 76110
(817) 926-3333
www.akropolis.net/members/inside

Interior Decisions, Inc.
140 Columbia Turnpike
Florham Park, NJ 07932
(973) 765-9013
www.interiordecisions.com

Interiors by Decorating Den™
Anne M. Fawcett
551 Adams St.
Milton, MA 02186
(617) 698-8303
www.decoratingden.com

Interiors by Decorating Den™
Rose Bucheri
2224 Armeda Way
San Mateo, CA 94404
(650) 571-5610

Jan Kyle Design
4946 Belinder Rd.
Westwood, Kansas 66205
(913) 677-3290

Joan Nemirow Designs, LLC
16 Woodcock Ln.
Westport, CT 06880
(203) 222-7504

Joseph Hittinger Designs
378 Cambridge Ave., Ste. B
Palo Alto, CA 94306
(650) 322-8388
www.josephhittingerdesigns.com

KAA Design Group
4201 Redwood Ave.
Los Angeles, CA 90066
(310) 821-1400
www.kaadesigngroup.com

Kitchen Concepts, Inc.
159 Washington St.
Norwell, MA 02061
(781) 878-6542
www.roomscapesinc.com

Kitchens by Design of Sarasota
4233 Clark Rd.
Sarasota, FL 34233
(941) 924-7067

Kitchens By Kleweno
4034 Broadway
Kansas City, MO 64111
(816) 531-3968
www.kleweno.com

Krumdieck A+I Design, Inc.
2226 1st Ave. South
Birmingham, AL 35233
(205) 324-9669
www.krumdieck.com

L.D. Burke Designs
2 Riverdale Ave.
Monmouth Beach, NJ 07750
(732) 229-8200

Lark Interiors
27 Wistar Rd.
Paoli, PA 19301
(610) 889-9981
www.larkinteriors.com

Lisa Leigh Johnson Interior Design
Studio
Traverse City, MI
Milwaukee, WI
(414) 403-4100
www.lisainteriordesigns.com
migrationhome.com

Marcy Voyevod Design
110 Linden St.
Oakland, CA 94607
(510) 433-0724
www.marcyvoyevod.com

Miller / Dolezal Design Group
3000 Alpine Rd.
Portola Valley, CA 94028
(650) 529-2700
www.millerdolezal.com

Miller Stein Interior Design
4546 El Camino Real, Ste. B5
Los Altos, CA 94022
(650) 559-1705
www.millerstein.com

Morgan House Interiors
42 Main St., Ste. 6
Clinton, NJ, 08809
(908) 735-6654
www.morganhouseinteriors.com

Patricia McLean Interiors, Inc.
3179 Maple Dr., Ste. 8 & 10
Atlanta, GA 30305
(404) 266-9772
www.mcleaninteriors.com

Plain & Fancy Custom Cabinetry
Oak St. & Rt. 501
Schaefferstown, PA 17088
(800) 447-9006
www.plainfancycabinetry.com

SJ Designs
824 Arlington Road
Redwood City, CA 94062
(650) 365-3433

Showplace Design & Remodeling, Inc.
8710 Willows Rd.
Redmond, WA 98052
(425) 885-1595
www.showplaceinc.com

Talents Design Studio, Inc.
3841 East Edison Place
Tucson, AZ 85716
(520) 326-1172

Torrell Architects
1121 Pike St.
Seattle, WA 98101
(206) 264-7777

Umphrey Interiors
1225 51st St. S.
Birmingham, AL 35222
(205) 422-6969

Weatherly Tile & Stone, Inc.
3030 East Main Rd.
Portsmouth, RI 02871
(401) 683-5577
www.weatherlytile.com

MORE SCHIFFER TITLES

www.schifferbooks.com

Big Book of Kitchen Design Ideas. Tina Skinner. More than 300 big, full-color photographs of stunning kitchens provide an encyclopedic resource of design ideas for homeowners, designers, and contractors. The kitchen designs presented here include award winning designs and fancy product showcases designed for many of the nation's leading manufacturers of cabinetry, countertops, windows, appliances, and floors. Many styles of kitchens are covered, from contemporary and country, to classic European looks, early American, retro, and art deco designs. Special needs are addressed for elderly and handicapped users, as well as design issues faced by families with young children. There are designs for people who entertain frequently, and for those who need the kitchen to serve every purpose—from home office to dining room, to laundry room."The book is designed as a reference library for the do-it-yourselfer, or as a bank of illustrations to share with a designer or contractor when seeking the right look for your old or new home. A reference guide at the back of the book lists manufacturers and designers ready and eager to help you on your way to creating the perfect heart for your home."

Size: 8 1/2" x 11"   321 color photos   144pp.
ISBN: 0-7643-0672-3   soft cover $24.95

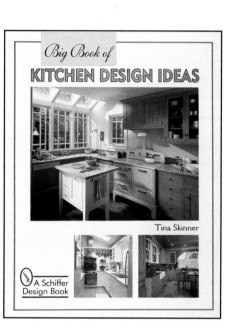

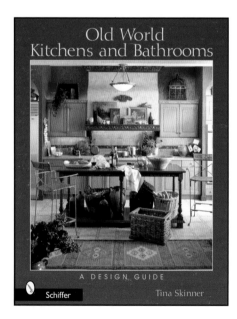

Old World Kitchens and Bathrooms: A Design Guide. Tina Skinner. This book captures today's hottest design trend for the home - textures, design, colors, and craftsmanship that evoke European ideals of a bygone era. Explore kitchens and baths rich in the fine details that characterize Provencal, Tuscan, and English country designs. Massive range hoods and brick hearths, faux finishes, rich natural stone, and tile provide polish and posh to up-to-the-minute home environments. Enjoy hand-carved wood, wrought-iron, and fine crystal chandeliers in spaces filled with the latest appliances and an abundance of workspace. The atmosphere is timeless, and these designs are certain to endure. This is an indispensable design guide for professional designers and discerning homeowners.

ISBN: 8 1/2" x 11"   112pp.
ISBN: 0-7643-2078-5   soft cover $19.95

Schiffer books may be ordered from your local bookstore, or they may be ordered directly from the publisher by writing to:
Schiffer Publishing, Ltd.
4880 Lower Valley Rd
Atglen PA 19310
(610) 593-1777; Fax (610) 593-2002
E-mail: Info@schifferbooks.com

Please visit our web site catalog at *www.schifferbooks.com* or write for a free catalog. Please include $3.95 for shipping and handling for the first two books and $1.00 for each additional book. Free shipping for orders $100 or more.

Printed in China